QUESTIONS IN HISTORY

SERIES EDITOR: ALAN WHITE

STALIN'S RUSSIA

Martyn Whittock

To my good friends, Alison and Tim Bird

Published by CollinsEducational
An imprint of HarperCollins*Publishers*
77–85 Fulham Palace Road
London W6 8JB

© HarperCollins*Publishers* 1997

First published 1997
Reprinted 1997

ISBN 0 00 327277-X

British Library Cataloguing in Publication Data

A catalogue record for this book is available from the British Library.

Acknowledgements

I would like to thank a number of people who have assisted me in the writing of this book. Martin Crouch, lecturer in The Development of the Soviet State at Bristol University, first fired my interest in the history of the USSR. My Sixth Form classes of 1996 and 1997 at Kingdown School, Warminster, debated with me many of the issues central to this study (thanks especially to Tom Jefferson, first of the 'New Realists' and to the 'Babes'). Steve Tamplin kindly trialed material at Queen Elizabeth's School, Dorset and Ann Trivett did the same at Backwell, Somerset. I am particularly grateful to Lord Bullock who assisted me with valuable personal comments and insights on the theme of political interpretations.

The author and publishers would like to thank the following for permission to reproduce illustrations:

David King Collection (pp. 20, 40, 41)

Cover photograph: 'Stalin at the map' by F. Reshetnikov; Society for Co-operation in Russian and Soviet Studies.

Edited by Lorimer Poultney
Design by Derek Lee
Artwork by Hardlines
Production by Susan Cashin

Printed and bound by
Scotprint Limited, Musselburgh

Contents

1 Why did Stalin win the struggle for power?

The Communist Party in the 1920s, Stalin's rise to power and the defeat of his rivals

---

Key points

- ◆ The Communist Party in the early 1920s
- ◆ How and why was the Left Opposition defeated?
- ◆ The defeat of the Right Deviation
- ◆ Trotsky: more weaknesses than strengths?
- ◆ Why did Stalin win the struggle for power?

The Communist Party in the early 1920s: what factors influenced the power struggle?

When Lenin died in January 1924 he left no clear successor to lead the Communist Party. Indeed, it seemed obvious at the time that no one person could play the same leading role that he had. Instead a group of leaders emerged, a 'collective leadership'. By 1929, however, one of these leaders, Stalin, had defeated the others and had become the dominant force in the politics of the USSR. His success was as a result of a power struggle which had started before Lenin's death. It was a power struggle, whose character was affected by a number of important factors.

The ban on factionalism

At the Tenth Party Congress, held in March 1921, a resolution had been passed that had banned all groups within the Party which tried to put forward ideas disagreeing with official policy and the Party leadership. People who resisted could be expelled from the Party. A secret clause – not revealed until January 1924 – allowed the leadership to expel any members of the Party who showed lack of discipline, or who showed a "tolerance of factionalism". This applied to all Party members, even those on the ruling Central Committee of the Party.

This was important because it limited the amount of debate within the Party. It also meant that anyone who persisted in criticising official Party ideas could be expelled. During the power struggle of the 1920s those who succeeded in getting their ideas accepted by the Party congresses and the Central Committee were quick to accuse their opponents of 'factionalism'.

A centralised Party machine

Traditionally, leading Communists disapproved of bureaucracy in government. The idea of centralised power dominated by civil servants and paperwork did not appeal to revolutionaries. However, after the 1917 revolution the Party rapidly found that dealing with the complexities of government forced it to become more centralised. Dr Edward Acton has noted "the speed with which the Party forfeited mass support in the aftermath of the revolution and shifted its powerbase from Soviet democracy to administrative and military coercion" (*Rethinking the Russian Revolution*, 1990).

One of the aspects of this growing complexity and centralisation was the setting up of a Party Secretariat which had the job of organising the running of the Party, ensuring that decisions were carried out and appointing people to essential jobs. Until 1919 this work had been carried out by Jacob Sverdlov and a tiny staff of 15. With his death the work was reorganised. As the Party became the most powerful force within the country this part of the Party organisation became more and more important, though few people foresaw how influential it would become.

Stalin became General Secretary of the Party in April 1922, though he had been doing a similar job since 1919 at Rabkrin (the Workers' and Peasants' Inspectorate). This position and the growing centralisation of the Party put him in a unique position to influence job appointments and the Party organisation.

The growth in Party membership

Following Lenin's death a campaign was mounted to increase the size of the Party. Called the 'Lenin enrolment' the number of members doubled in two years from less than half a million to over a million. By 1933 membership had reached three and a half million.

Many of these new members – called the '*Lenintsy*' – were young, inexperienced and poorly educated. By 1927 less than 8% of the Party's members had been to secondary school. These people were more likely to obey instructions from the Party leaders than older, more experienced revolutionaries would. They owed their membership and jobs to the Secretariat which oversaw the Lenin enrolment. They were "malleable recruits" (L. Schapiro, T*he Communist Party of the Soviet U*nion, 1970), who were, as Alan Bullock has concluded, "ready enough to accept what they were told" (H*itler and Stalin*, 1991).

No one clear leader

Lenin dominated the Communist Party by the force of his personality and ideas. He did not occupy an official position as leader. He chaired the meetings of the Politburo – the supreme governing group of the Party – and was chairman of the Council of Peoples' Commissars – the government. However, he did not have one clear position which combined these roles.

When Lenin suffered his first stroke, in May 1922, there was no obvious way to replace him and no one person in a position to do so if there had been a way.

This was made more complex by Lenin's Testament. Produced between December 1922 and January 1923 it was Lenin's last message to the Party. In it he criticised all the leading candidates for running the Party after his death. Stalin he described as not being able to use "power with sufficient caution"; Trotsky was criticised for "excessive self-assurance and excessive absorption in administration"; Bukharin could not be regarded as "fully Marxist"; Zinoviev and Kamenev were criticised for lack of enthusiasm for the Bolshevik seizure of power in October 1917. Later, Lenin added a note attacking Stalin as "too rude" and proposing that he should lose his job as General Secretary.

The importance of Lenin's Testament is that it damaged everyone. It was probably intended to ensure that no one leader emerged and that the leading Party members worked together. He hoped that these leaders would be controlled by the Central Committee, the body which effectively ran the Party and which Lenin hoped to make more representative of the Party membership. However, the wording of the Testament also had the effect of making sure that none of those competing for power had an interest in publishing it. This meant that Lenin's final fears about Stalin were effectively ignored.

How was the Left Opposition defeated?

Lenin's strokes removed him from active participation in government from May 1922. Between then and his death, in January 1924, the leading members of the Party began to compete for control. They were all members of the Politburo. These leading members were:

◆ Stalin, General Secretary, Commissar for Nationalities (until 1923) and Commissar for State Control (also until 1923).

◆ Trotsky, Commissar for War, who had played the major part in organising the victorious Red Army in the Civil War.

◆ Zinoviev, head of the Party organisation in Petrograd (later Leningrad) and chairman of the Comintern, which co-ordinated world Communist parties.

◆ Kamenev, chairman of the Moscow Soviet and deputy Chairman of the Council of Peoples' Commissars. He also acted as chairman of the Politburo in Lenin's absence.

◆ Bukharin, editor of the Party newspaper, *Pravda*. He became a full member of the Politburo after Lenin's death.

The alliance against Trotsky

Stalin, Zinoviev and Kamenev feared Trotsky. He was a brilliant thinker, speaker and organiser. He was nationally famous and had been Lenin's right-hand man. Trotsky later claimed that Lenin had groomed him as his successor by suggesting that he take the job of Deputy Chairman of the Council of Peoples' Commissars. However, Trotsky had turned the job down – the first of many political blunders and lack of foresight.

Despite this, Trotsky was the man most feared by the other senior members of the Politburo. They formed a three-person alliance against him – a 'troika'.

In 1923 at the Twelfth Party Congress Trotsky refused to make the principal speech in Lenin's place (Lenin, still alive, was too ill to attend). He seemed to have been reluctant to be seen as competing for power. Later he wrote that "if I had come forward on the eve of the Twelfth Congress in the spirit of a bloc of Lenin and Trotsky against the Stalin bureaucracy, I should have been victorious". The important thing is that he did not! He refused to compete and instead it was Stalin who dominated the Congress.

At the same Congress Stalin skilfully appeared to agree with Lenin's complaints about Russians trying to dominate other nationalities in the USSR. These complaints had been aimed at Stalin but he made it appear that he agreed with them. Trotsky knew the truth and had been asked by Lenin to take up the case of Communists in Georgia (who felt Stalin was bullying them). Trotsky could have "blown Stalin out of the water" (L. Schapiro, *The Communist Party of the Soviet Union*, 1970) but did not even attend the debate. Such opportunities to weaken Stalin would not come twice.

Stalin's increasingly powerful position worried Zinoviev, but when Stalin offered to resign, Zinoviev backed off as he was more concerned about Trotsky.

In October Trotsky published an open letter to the Central Committee, attacking the government's economic policy and accusing Stalin's Secretariat of controlling elections within the Party. Later that month he organised 'The Declaration of the Forty-Six', a similar attack signed by leading critics of those dominating the government. Trotsky's tactics left him wide open to the accusation of 'factionalism'. He was condemned by the Central Committee, which was dominated by his opponents. Trotsky had previously supported Lenin's rules on factions and was now caught by his opponents using the same tactics against him.

A mystery illness caused him to miss this meeting of the Central Committee. This would be a recurring pattern and may well have resulted from his unwillingness to really seize the initiative. In December 1923 he again attacked the way the Party was run and then, with a recurrence of his 'illness', left Moscow for a holiday. This meant he missed another Central Committee meeting in January 1924 which openly censured the "Trotsky faction".

Similarly Trotsky was absent for Lenin's funeral. He claimed he had been told the wrong date by the Politburo but in reality seems to have lacked the political will to fight for the leadership position. In his absence, Stalin presented himself as the loyal disciple of Lenin.

The defeat of Trotsky

In May 1924 the Central Committee decided not to publish Lenin's Testament. Zinoviev and Kamenev opposed publishing because it might have been to the advantage of Trotsky. Trotsky said nothing! In October 1924 Trotsky published *The Lessons of October* in which he attacked Zinoviev and Kamenev. This suggests he still regarded them, rather than Stalin, as his main enemies.

The troika used this as a signal to turn on Trotsky. He was accused of inventing 'Trotskyism', which it was suggested was not in line with Lenin's beliefs. This accusation was encouraged by his earlier tactics which had caused him to appear as a factionalist. As part of this process of neutralising him, Trotsky was accused of believing in 'permanent revolution'. This, it was claimed, meant that socialism could not be built in the USSR until revolution had spread to western Europe. In fact, Lenin had believed much the same thing but now Stalin and his supporters declared the possibility of 'socialism in one country'. This suggested that the USSR could achieve socialism despite the failure of the revolution to spread. It was a positive and popular suggestion. It made Trotsky sound negative and appeared to suggest that he differed from Lenin, which he did not!

Trotsky made no attempt to respond to the criticisms made against *Lessons of October*. In January 1925 he was again condemned by the Central Committee. He was again not present due to 'illness' and resigned as Commissar for War. At this meeting Stalin opposed moves by Zinoviev and Kamenev to expel

Trotsky from the Party. Throughout this period Stalin frequently took a very moderate position.

Trotsky seems to have experienced one of his bouts of political paralysis during 1925. His only major act was to condemn a US publication of parts of Lenin's Testament. Trotsky followed the official Party line and denied the Testament existed.

Conflict between Stalin, Zinoviev and Kamenev

With Trotsky badly weakened, Stalin moved against Zinoviev and Kamenev. Using his influence within the Party organisation he undermined Zinoviev's position as Chairman of the Comintern (he lost the position during 1926); Kamenev lost control of the Party organisation in Moscow. However, attempts by Stalin to place his own people in the Leningrad Party organisation led to resistance from Zinoviev.

During 1925 Zinoviev counter-attacked against Stalin. He attacked the leadership's support for the New Economic Policy (NEP). This relaxation of Communist control over the peasantry had been introduced by Lenin in 1921 and was not popular in large parts of the Party. Trotsky had earlier argued in favour of rapid industrialisation and now Zinoviev used the same argument in order to try to rally support behind himself. In particular he attacked Bukharin who had become an enthusiastic supporter of the NEP.

Stalin was in favour of increased industrialisation too but formed an alliance with Bukharin to defeat Zinoviev and his ally Kamenev. When the Fourteenth Party Congress met in December 1925 Stalin's supporters easily defeated Zinoviev and Kamenev. The Congress representatives "nominally elected by their Party constituencies, had been hand-picked by the Party organisations" (E. H. Carr, *The Russian Revolution From Lenin to Stalin*, 1979). During 1926 Zinoviev lost control of Leningrad; Kamenev lost all his government posts and ceased to be a full member of the Politburo, now dominated by supporters of Stalin.

The defeat of the United Opposition

In 1926 Trotsky, Zinoviev and Kamenev joined forces in an attempt to fight back against Stalin. They formed the 'United Opposition', a strange alliance of formerly bitter enemies. Unable to control the Party 'machine', their actions were too late and made them appear like the outsiders they had become. Lacking support in the Central Committee, they held protest meetings, then retreated in the face of intimidation organised by Party members who owed their jobs to Stalin.

In October they supplied copies of Lenin's Testament to the world press. It was a desperate action by defeated people. It was also too late. In response the Central Committee removed Trotsky, Zinoviev and Kamenev from all positions of power. In the autumn of 1927 the secret police banned opposition leaflets and – when the ban was ignored – raided their printing plants. Street demonstrations were broken up by the police and Party gangs.

The Opposition, with no control over the Party machine, could only act outside of it as factionalists. Trotsky, Zinoviev and Kamenev were expelled from the Party. Zinoviev and Kamenev were later allowed back in, their power destroyed. In January 1928 Trotsky was exiled to Central Asia; in January 1929 he was expelled from the USSR. He was never to return.

The defeat of the Right Deviation: principles without a powerbase?

The so–called 'Left Opposition' had attacked the NEP and argued for rapid industrialisation. Stalin, though he had defended the NEP in order to present the opposition as factionalists attacking Party policy, was no enthusiast for the NEP either. He too was committed to increased industrialisation and was careful to distance himself from Bukharin, who was a more enthusiastic supporter of the NEP and its alliance with the peasants.

With the defeat of the United Opposition Stalin changed direction. It was now possible to criticise the NEP without helping the opposition. This change left Bukharin and his allies Rykov and Tomsky dangerously exposed. Not only did they not control the Party machine but they were supporters of a policy which was not popular within the Party. Unlike Zinoviev, Kamenev and Trotsky, Bukharin was not in a position to really resist Stalin. He lacked a powerbase and could rapidly be undermined.

A crisis in the amount of grain harvested in 1927 was met with increasing force, designed to take grain from peasants who were thought to be hoarding it. From January 1928 this campaign of forced grain requisitioning was led by Stalin and culminated in the collectivisation of Soviet agriculture. It also culminated in the total defeat of Bukharin. In July 1928 he secretly visited his old enemy Kamenev, claiming that Stalin "has made concessions only so that he can cut our throats later". To his record of the meeting Kamenev added, "Stalin knows only one method . . . to plant a knife in the back." The Right conducted its resistance within the Politburo, fearful of the charge of factionalism. Consequently it was never able to organise a real campaign of resistance across the Party and probably could not have inspired one if it had tried to do so.

In November 1929 Bukharin was expelled from the Politburo and lost his position at the Comintern, where he had replaced Zinoviev. Earlier his ally Tomsky had lost his Trade Union powerbase. The Right Deviation, as it had been labelled, was not significant enough to be granted the title of 'Opposition'. The power struggle was over. "Like previous oppositions to Stalin the Right was defeated by the Party machine which Stalin controlled" (S. Fitzpatrick, *The Russian Revolution* 1917–1932, 1982).

Trotsky: more weaknesses than strengths?

Trotsky had great strengths which made him appear a strong candidate to replace Lenin. He was a brilliant intellectual, took much of the credit for the Civil War victory and was close to Lenin. This position of the obvious successor has been enhanced by a number of factors: Trotsky's own writings in exile, the fact that it suited Stalin to make him appear the arch villain in the 1930s, the support of Trotskyist writers and sympathisers in the West. However, it can be argued that his strengths have been greatly overrated and that he at no point offered a credible alternative to Stalin.

Despite his fame, he had no real powerbase in the Party and nothing to compare with Stalin's. Indeed, his Menshevik origins and rather difficult personality lend credence to the assessment that "the only role open to him was as a critic of his party" (M. Reiman, *The Trotsky Reappraisal*, 1992). His flamboyant personality led many to fear him as a 'Bonapartist' leader who would seize personal control of the Revolution, when the real danger lay in the less extrovert Stalin. He had also been willing to stifle the free speech of others that he – and Lenin – regarded as factionalists, but protested when the same methods were used against himself. Additionally his arguments for applying military discipline to workers during the Civil War had lost him support amongst the working class. In many ways his power came from his close relationship with Lenin. The death of Lenin left him vulnerable to attack.

Perhaps most important is his failure to really 'compete'. He seems to have been unable to bring himself to take on his opponents with consistent effort. His actions were often too late, lacking in energy and poorly planned (given the Party's obsession with factionalism). His grand gestures did little to threaten his enemies and much to undermine his own position. His illnesses seem curious manifestations of a personal crisis which made him fail to rise to the occasion and fight for power.

Why did Stalin win the struggle for power?

Stalin's victory was not inevitable, nor was it a result of his political skills alone. A whole web of factors combined to assist his victory:

◆ The centralised nature of the Party made it relatively easy to control through the Secretariat. This had begun under Lenin.

◆ The opposition to 'factionalism', established by Lenin, led Zinoviev, Kamenev and Bukharin to sanction treatment of their enemies which was later used against themselves. The same had earlier been true of Trotsky. "The defeat of each successive opposition violently narrowed the margins within which free expression was possible" (I. Deutscher, *Stalin*, 1966).

◆ Poorly educated new Party members were easy to dominate.

◆ Many Party members desired radical change which made it easy to isolate Bukharin and attack the NEP.

◆ Stalin's opponents made major errors: failure to publish Lenin's Testament; underestimating Stalin and exaggerating the danger presented by Trotsky; poor tactics which appeared factional; lack of determined struggle (i.e. Trotsky's inconsistencies).

◆ Stalin's own political skills. He appeared a moderate for much of the time; shifted his position to make others appear as factionalists; used his position to place 'his people' in key jobs; he was willing to use increasing force, such as the OGPU secret police, against the United Opposition.

Studying 'The power struggle'

1 In identifying the strengths and weaknesses of the contenders in the power struggle it can help to build up a 'potted' biography of Stalin, Trotsky, Zinoviev, Kamenev and Bukharin up to 1921. Include their main achievements and positions held in the Party. Also include areas of weakness which might affect their performance in a struggle for power.

2 "Stalin won the power struggle less because of his own skills and more because of the mistakes made by others." To what extent is this an accurate assessment?

2 Collectivisation

Economic necessity, or the settlement of old scores with the peasantry?

Key points

◆ Why did Stalin abandon the NEP?
◆ Was the grain procurement crisis the inevitable consequences of NEP, or product of government inflexibility?
◆ Was collectivisation a rural revolution, or a disaster?

Why did Stalin abandon the NEP?

During 1928 Stalin abandoned the New Economic Policy which had dominated Soviet economy and society for most of the 1920s. It was replaced with the forced collectivisation of agriculture. This was a move with far-reaching consequences which, linked to rapid industrialisation, had profound results.

What was the New Economic Policy?

The New Economic Policy was introduced by Lenin in 1921. It replaced War Communism, a term which was invented at the time of the NEP's introduction to describe the previous government handling of the economy. Unlike War Communism, the NEP promised a more relaxed relationship between the Communist government and the peasants and other small-scale businesses.

The previous policy had been associated with forced seizures of grain, collective punishments of villages that failed to meet grain delivery targets and strict controls on trade. This policy had been immensely unpopular in the countryside during the Civil War and had been a contributory factor in bringing the economy to the brink of collapse. The NEP was an attempt to stimulate the economy again by encouraging private enterprise. It replaced forced grain seizures with a fixed tax and allowed peasants to sell their surpluses for a profit. The NEP also saw the growth of independent small businesses and a general recovery in the economy.

Although the NEP was a retreat for the Communist Party it was not accompanied by any political relaxation. The Communist Party kept political power firmly within its own hands and the largest industries – the 'commanding heights' – remained in state control. As Lenin put it: "Let the peasants have their little bit of capitalism, as long as we keep the power."

Problems with the NEP

The NEP was not without its problems. In the so-called 'scissors crisis' of 1923–24, low production of industrial goods caused their prices to rise, whilst prices for agricultural products fell. Peasants lost the incentive to produce crops. Although an improvement in industrial output helped resolve this crisis, critics of the NEP, such as Trotsky, argued that the only long-term answer was greater state control of the economy and the expansion of industry.

As important a problem was the fact that the NEP was not acceptable to most members of the Communist Party. At the NEP's introduction Lenin had insisted that "We were forced to resort to War Communism by war and ruin. It was a temporary measure." However, many in his party did not see it this way and Lenin presented it in this light to make a change to the NEP more acceptable. In reality there is strong evidence to suggest that what he later called the 'temporary' measure of War Communism, for all its complex and contradictory nature, was "essentially the policy of victorious Communism" (E. Mawdsley, *The Russian Civil War*, 1987)

The NEP, then, was a real retreat in ideological terms. In many ways it was a betrayal of the natural inclinations of the Party, which opposed private property and profit and which regarded the peasantry as unreliable and a dangerous source of capitalist tendencies. The limited nature of the relaxation under the NEP was not able to allay fears about the retreat as "even a partial revival of capitalism was offensive and frightening to most Party members" (S. Fitzpatrick, *The Russian Revolution*, 1917–32, 1982).

During the NEP the state cut back its involvement in health care and reduced benefits and expenditure on education. At the same time urban unemployment rose, which fuelled working-class dissatisfaction. This dissatisfaction was frequently focused on middle-class managers, many of whom maintained positions of authority that they had held before the Revolution. Working-class antagonism towards these '*spetsy*' (specialists) was aggravated by the fact that they felt their own position and influence had been greatly reduced by the NEP.

The Communist Party could not ignore growing resentment amongst its own members and the working class in general. If the NEP was a retreat, the question arose as to how long such a retreat should go on for? By the mid-1920s the more radical voices in the Party were beginning to argue that the time had come to return to more revolutionary politics.

Stalin and industrialisation

During the power struggle of the 1920s attacks on the NEP and calls for rapid industrialisation were at first associated with Trotsky and the Left Opposition; criticisms of government policy which by 1925 had attracted Zinoviev and Kamenev too. Although the division between contenders for the leadership of the Party was real enough, there was actually no major difference between them over the need to industrialise the USSR. Whilst it suited Stalin to adopt a more moderate position towards the NEP until the Left and United Oppositions were defeated, he signalled his commitment to rapid industrial growth as early as 1925. Even while he was defending Bukharin – a keen supporter of NEP – from the attacks of the United Opposition, Stalin was careful not to tie himself too closely to a policy that had so little support in the Party.

In 1925 the Party Congress decided to press forward with a Five-Year Plan. Stalin associated himself strongly with this measure, which was popular in the

Party and which promised a bold step forward, comparable to the October Revolution itself. The Five-Year Plans did not inevitably mean the end of the NEP, but the need for massive state intervention and extraction of huge amounts of grain to pay for industrial growth meant that the delicate balance of the NEP could easily be destroyed.

Stalin's eventual abandonment of the NEP was not just a cynical ploy to destroy Bukharin and steal the beliefs of the defeated Left and United Oppositions. It clearly had this effect and this was probably one of his motives but it is a mistake to assume this was his only motive. Stalin had never been wholeheartedly in favour of the NEP. He was committed to industrialisation and was well aware of the unpopularity of the NEP within the Party. A genuine desire, on his part, to launch a radical transformation of the USSR, which would harness the enthusiasm of the Party and the workers, was as important a motive as a desire to defeat his political opponents.

The grain procurement crisis – the options

From 1925 the Communist Party was committed to rapid industrialisation of the USSR. This would involve a huge expenditure of money, as many of the machines and products to make it possible would have to be purchased from outside the USSR. How was this to be paid for?

◆ Take the necessary money (the capital) from the middle classes.

◆ Borrow money from abroad.

◆ Encourage greater grain production by increasing prices paid by the state to peasants; then sell grain abroad and buy machinery with the money received. Greater peasant efficiency could be achieved by encouraging them to join larger agricultural units (collective farms) which shared machinery and other scarce technical resources.

◆ Take grain from the peasants by force and make them join collective farms. These would be controlled by the state in order to ensure the maximum output of grain and other agricultural products.

The first two options were non-starters. The old middle class had lost most of its wealth as a result of the Revolution. Those who had prospered under the NEP – the so-called 'NEPmen' – had not had time to accumulate enough wealth for the state to seize. The political isolation of the USSR made it hard to borrow sufficient capital from abroad. Indeed from 1927 relations with a number of other states deteriorated to such a degree that there was a real fear of war in the USSR.

The answer seemed to lie in the last two options. The difference between them was whether force, or persuasion, should be applied to the peasantry. In the mid 1920s this was the subject of a debate between Bukharin and one of the Opposition, Preobrazhensky. Preobrazhensky argued that it would be necessary to adopt strict measures against the peasants in order to extract the maximum amount of grain. Bukharin objected to this. He said it would alienate the peasants and would break the worker–peasant alliance which Lenin had made the basis of the NEP. The debate did not reach a conclusion. Bukharin wanted to industrialise but was not clear how the huge amount of grain would be collected. Preobrazhensky agreed that violence should be avoided.

The problem of the kulaks

The state's options were not helped by Bolshevik distrust of the peasantry. There was a strong feeling within the Party that the peasants could not be counted on to increase grain production voluntarily. Or if they did, it would only be because the state had been forced to raise the price of grain to an unacceptable level.

Urban Communists believed that the problem was caused by rich peasants who controlled the greatest part of the wealth in the countryside. These peasants were called '*kulaks*', from a Russian word meaning 'fist/grasping'. If these kulaks could be removed then the majority of peasants would willingly join the collective farms and increase grain production. These other peasants were called the 'middle peasants' and the 'poor peasants'.

However, the reality was not so simple. There were in fact very few rich peasants. In 1927 they made up no more than 3.9% of the rural population. Only 2% of the rural population hired labourers, while on the other hand only 4% were so poor that they had no access to village land. This demonstrates that the official Party view that the countryside was made up of suffering peasants exploited by a large group of rural capitalists was false. In fact, 62.7% of the rural population were independent-minded 'middle peasants', who enjoyed a reasonable standard of living. Any attack on so-called kulaks was likely to fall on these middle peasants. This was especially true because there was no genuine desire to join collective farms and during the Civil War it had become clear that most peasants regarded the urban Communists as outsiders (see Orlando Figes, A *People's Tragedy*, 1996).

Any attempt to force Party policy on the peasants was likely to meet determined and united resistance from a broad range of peasants.

The effect of Communist ideology on available options

The Party image of the countryside meant that a compromise with the peasantry was unacceptable. Such a compromise would appear to reward the kulaks. It would appear to be accepting the backward state of Soviet agriculture and the fact that the peasants were not really under Communist control. The Communist Party, already disillusioned with the NEP, was not ideologically disposed to increase grain prices in order to encourage greater production.

A combination of the need to increase grain production, the Party's view of the class composition of the countryside and the deep distrust of all peasants and of the NEP made a conflict almost inevitable. When, despite a good harvest in 1927, the amount of grain bought by the state fell, the only explanation acceptable to the government was that kulaks were hoarding it; the reason they were doing this was to force prices up. They were holding the state to ransom. In fact the war scare of 1927 and the low prices paid for grain probably lay behind the shortage. Prices paid by the government had been reduced in 1926. However, the grain procurement crisis made the state appear weak and undermined its industrialisation plans.

Party ideology made a compromise difficult to justify. There were alternatives to conflict but none were acceptable to the majority in the Party leadership. Stalin was not alone in the desire to finally impose Communist control on the countryside; to settle scores with 'unreliable' and 'rebellious' peasants.

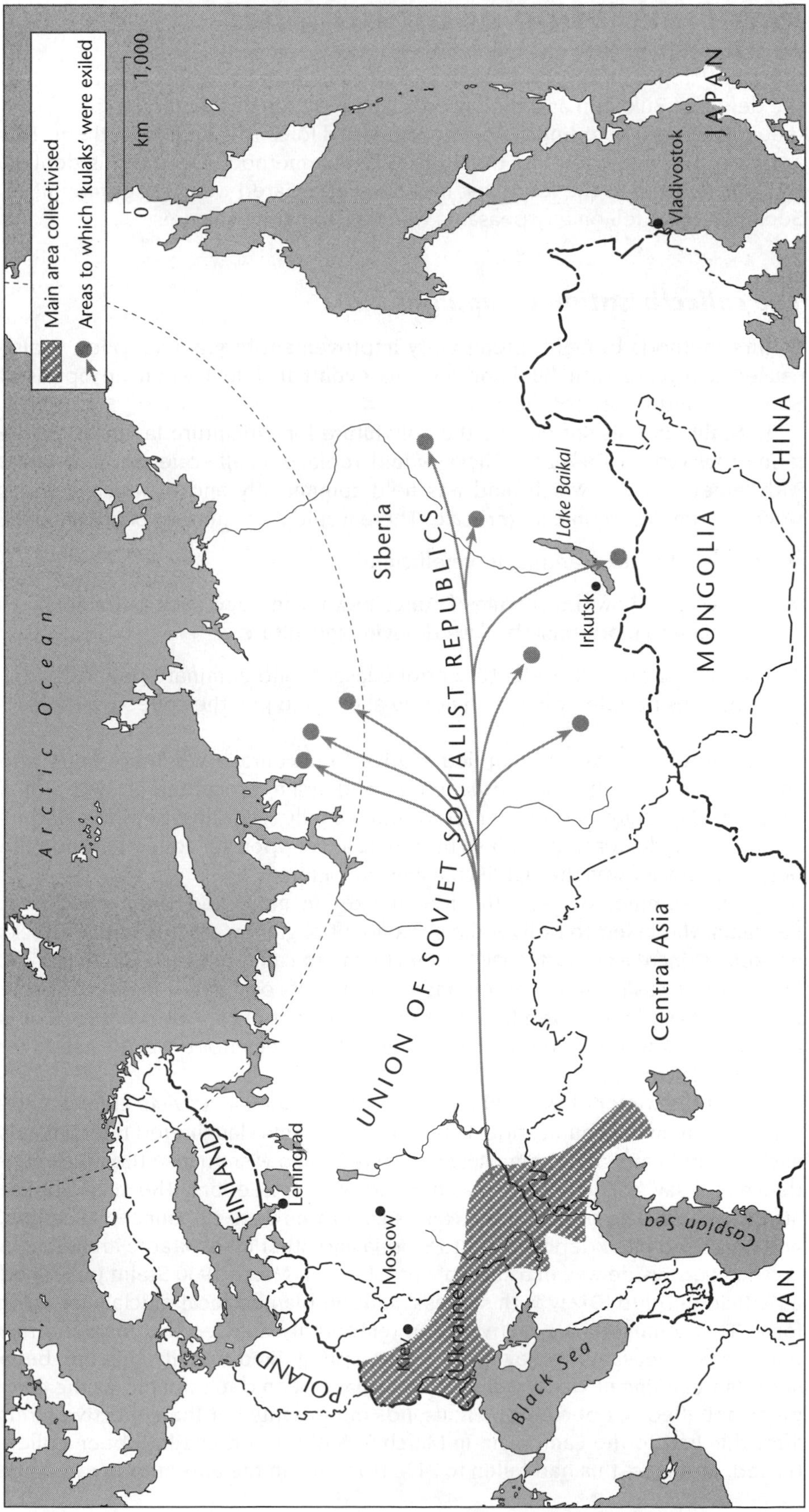

Figure 1

The main areas of the USSR collectivised during 1928–1932, and places of exile for opponents of the campaigns.

Rural revolution or catastrophe?

In early 1928 Stalin visited Siberia and began a process which was to lead to the defeat of Bukharin and the forced collectivisation of agriculture. Convinced that kulaks were hoarding grain he encouraged force to take it from them. This approach became known as the 'Urals-Siberian method'. Despite his denials, this was a return to the force that had been associated with War Communism. Soon that force fell on any peasants who resisted grain seizures.

The collectivisation campaigns

Stalin's methods brought a temporary improvement in grain supplies. It also caused a rupture with Bukharin and his eventual defeat when he opposed Stalin's abandonment of the NEP.

To Stalin and his supporters the only future for agriculture lay in collective farms ('*kolkhozi*' in Russian). These would replace small-scale peasant farms with larger units, in which land was held communally and in which peasant work was organised on a larger scale. There would be a number of advantages:

◆ They would make farming more efficient.

◆ They would allow the sharing of scarce new technology, such as tractors, necessary to modernise backward Soviet agriculture.

◆ They would make it easier to control peasants and eliminate politically dangerous people, who would not be allowed to join the collective farms.

In the winter of 1928–29 Stalin led a drive to encourage voluntary entry into collective farms. This had little effect and grain procurement was still a problem. The state had now entered into a conflict with the peasants and its options were decreasing. With so little peasant support for collectivisation the only way forward was through increasing use of force.

By the summer of 1929 the free market in grain had been abolished. Peasants who failed to deliver the set amount of grain were punished. Attacks on 'kulaks' increased and Party leaders began to call for mass collectivisation. The process was gaining a radical momentum of its own and it is questionable how far it was planned and how far it ran almost out of control. What is clear is that Stalin allowed it to run and accelerated it. In December 1929 he called for the "liquidation of the kulaks as a class".

During the winter of 1929–30 thousands of Communist activists enforced collectivisation on the countryside. In response peasants slaughtered their animals and attacked Party members. Most peasants had no wish to lose their independence and saw collective farms as the end of their freedom. The secret police arrested those who opposed the campaign, or who were denounced as kulaks, and organised mass deportations to Siberia and other inhospitable areas.

The countryside was in a state of virtual war. In March 1930 Stalin published an article entitled 'Dizzy with success'. In it he blamed local officials for using force. This confused Party activists but temporarily diffused the crisis and this encouraged peasants to sow grain in the spring. Traditionally this has been seen as a cunning move by Stalin but may have been due to panic, as the campaign spiralled out of control. Thousands of peasants left the collective farms after this halt to the campaign. In March 50% of households had been collectivised; in August this had fallen to 21%. However, in the autumn the campaign began again and collectivisation was again imposed, assisted by volunteer Communists and workers who went out into the countryside (the 'Twenty-five thousanders'). By 1932 62% of peasant households were in collectives; by 1937 this had risen to 93%. Independent agriculture was no more.

The results of collectivisation

The seizure of grain did help to pay for industrial growth but this should not be exaggerated. It was not until 1937 that grain production again reached the pre-collectivisation amount, an indication of the chaos collectivisation caused. Judged purely from an economic point of view the result was disappointing. Livestock numbers collapsed, not recovering until the 1950s (see Appendix 2). However, to a Party which distrusted the growth of peasant capitalism this limited success seemed economically necessary and politically justifiable.

In the long-term Soviet agriculture was crippled. The productivity on collective farms was poor. By 1937, after the state had relented and again allowed peasants the right to own small private plots of land, over 50% of vegetables and 70% of milk came from these plots. These relics of free farming produced more than the whole collectivised sector, where peasants were subject to heavy taxation 'in kind' and had low living standards and low morale.

The human effects were catastrophic. In 1932–33 famine raged in southern Russia, while food was exported to pay for industrialisation. Latest analysis suggests between five and seven million people died as a result of the collectivisation famine. As well as this, by 1939 around 19 million people had left the countryside to work in towns and on construction projects. This though had a more positive effect, providing labour for the Five-Year Plans.

Politically the state was strengthened and firmly controlled the countryside. The process of collectivisation "served to brutalise and perhaps to atomise the rural population" (L. Viola, *Stalinist Terror, New Perspectives*, 1993). This made people less able to resist state demands and coercion. The secret police had agents in each local Machine Tractor Station, where technical equipment was kept for local *kolkhozi*. These became part of the control mechanism in a subdued countryside. The peasants, who had briefly seemed in a position to dictate policy to the Soviet state, had been crushed.

Collectivisation was therefore a combination of human catastrophe, debatable economic achievement and revolutionary change. It condemned Soviet agriculture to decades of stagnation. However, it also strengthened the state and provided labour for industrial growth. The fact outcomes were so mixed is no surprise, given the lack of clear planning behind the campaigns, which may be viewed as "a succession of crises as a result of hasty and ill-considered decisions" (A. Bullock, *Hitler and Stalin*, 1991)

Studying 'Collectivisation'

1 Make a list of Stalin's possible motives for collectivisation. Which do you think was the most important motive? Explain your choice.

2 Make a note of the results of the collectivisation campaigns under the headings: economic, political.

3 "Collectivisation was undoubtedly a real 'revolution from above' in the countryside." Do the results of collectivisation justify this conclusion?

How successful were the Five-Year Plans?

The industrialisation of the USSR

Key points

◆ What was the case for rapid industrialisation?
◆ Problems the state faced in implementing its plans
◆ Were the Five-Year Plans a success or a failure?

The case for rapid industrialisation?

In 1926 Stalin criticised Trotsky and the Left Opposition for their plans to industrialise the USSR. He scornfully described them as 'super-industrialisers' and attacked their plans for massive industrial growth as unrealistic and inappropriate. Even so, Stalin had already committed himself to supporting plans for industrialisation. At the eighth anniversary of the Revolution, in 1925, he had compared the Party's recent decision to press forward with a campaign of industrialisation with the 1917 Revolution itself.

Consequently his attacks on Trotsky should not be taken at face value. Stalin believed it was crucial to industrialise the USSR but during the power struggle it suited his purposes to combine this commitment with a wary support for the NEP. It was this, rather than any real doubts about the wisdom of rapidly improving the performance of Soviet industry, that lay behind his dismissal of the ideas of the Left Opposition. However, the case for a rapid industrialisation of the USSR was complex.

Communist ideology

The Communist Party had achieved power in an economically backward country. As Marxists, however, they believed that the revolutionary transformation of society would only come through industrialisation. Such a change would also dramatically increase the numbers of workers in the USSR. This was seen as crucial in a country where the majority of people were peasants, who had only a limited commitment to the regime. Consequently, the Party was ideologically and instinctively committed to the transformation of the USSR. Although there were disagreements over whether this process should emerge out of the NEP, or rapidly replace the NEP, the Party leadership, of all shades of opinion, accepted the inevitability of industrialisation. The only disagreement was over the timescale.

Harnessing the enthusiasm of the Soviet working class

The disillusionment felt by many in the Party and working class towards the NEP was a serious concern to the Soviet government. Among many of the more radical elements in both groups was a contempt for the backward nature of the USSR and a passionate belief in the virtues of modernisation. When Y. Olesha wrote in his novel *Envy* in 1927, that "I have become a human machine. It is what I want to be", he was expressing a widespread faith in modernisation and frustration with economic stagnation.

It was this frustration that the state diffused by adopting the Five-Year Plans. Yet by doing this the state did more than simply reduce dangerous dissatisfaction, it also harnessed the tremendous enthusiasm of many workers, especially the young. This was very important in building support for the government. This is why many of the targets and slogans of the Five-Year Plans were so dramatic. They went beyond mere economic planning and were intended to inspire and excite. They were in Ronald Hingley's phrase "magical and liturgical" (*Joseph Stalin: Man and Legend*, 1974).

Fear of war

During the mid- to late 1920s war scares in the USSR grew. In 1926 the right-wing Polish government broke off diplomatic relations with the USSR. Britain followed in 1927. By the late 1920s there were anti-Communist governments in Finland, Romania and Iran. The USSR regarded the Locarno Treaty as an attempt by the West to keep Germany from developing closer ties with the USSR.

In the Far East Soviet diplomacy faced serious setbacks when Russian advisers were arrested by the Nationalist Chinese in 1926 and when the Japanese government destroyed the Japanese Communist Party in 1927. The latter event took place as rivalry between the USSR and Japan over influence in Manchuria and Mongolia was increasing.

These developments increased the sense of isolation and vulnerability in the USSR. Given the backward nature of Soviet industry it seemed clear that the USSR could not hope to resist the attacks of a host of hostile nations. The only answer was to improve industrial capacity and strengthen the USSR. Such a policy would deter aggression and repel it if deterrence failed.

This motive for industrialisation is clearly paramount in an article of Stalin's, published in 1931: "Do you want our socialist fatherland to be beaten and to lose its independence? If you do not want this you must put an end to its backwardness . . . That is why Lenin said during the October Revolution: 'Either perish, or overtake and outstrip the advanced capitalist countries.' We are 50 or 100 years behind the advanced countries. We must make good this distance in ten years. Either we do it, or they crush us."

The defeat of Stalin's opponents

Stalin's commitment to the Five-Year Plans clearly had the effect of stealing the clothes of the Left and United Oppositions. It left Trotsky and Zinoviev with little that was distinctive about their beliefs. In addition, once they had been defeated, the shift towards very rapid industrialisation (coupled with collectivisation) was a tactic that isolated Bukharin. By achieving the industrialisation of the USSR Stalin's importance would also be comparable to that of Lenin.

Figure 2
'Seven problems – One Answer (The Five-Year Plan in Four Years).'

This poster, produced during the First Five-Year Plan (1928–33), makes it clear that defending the USSR from external threats was one of the motives behind rapid industrial-isation. With the exception of the Church, all the heads on the left of the poster represent foreign powers considered to be threatening the USSR.

It would be a mistake, however, to see Stalin's support for the Five-Year Plans as simply a cynical manoeuvre to wrong-foot his opponents. While it was clearly to his advantage to support industrialisation and this explains some-thing of the way in which his public support for it changed and developed, he was obviously a genuine believer in its necessity. Furthermore, he was responding to a strong pressure from within the Party. This was not something that he created, though he was skilful at manipulating it to his own advantage.

Contrast with the West

The Soviet commitment to economic growth and full employment was a stark contrast to the unemployment and waste so obvious in the West as the advanced capitalist countries sunk into global depression after the Wall Street Crash (1929). Such a contrast seemed to justify the USSR's claim that its ideol-ogy was superior to capitalism and capable of generating real growth and increased prosperity. While this did not stimulate the original commitment to the Five-Year Plans it clearly bolstered them and the dramatic claims made for their success.

What problems did the state face in implementing its Plans?

The details of the First Five-Year Plan were adopted by the Party in mid-1929. It was backdated to the previous October when it was considered to have begun. Its target was to increase dramatically the productivity of heavy industry (coal, iron, steel, engineering, etc.) in the USSR. It was finally declared to have been fulfilled in January 1933. It was followed by a Second Five-Year Plan (1933–37) and a Third Five-Year Plan, which began in 1937 but was cut short by the German invasion of the USSR in 1941. Each of the Plans had a slightly different focus for achievement. In embarking on rapid industrialisation the state faced a number of significant problems:

Waste and inefficiency

The scale and speed with which factories were built led to huge confusion. Machines were ordered and then left to rust. Workers were seen constructing tractors beside conveyor belts that should have supported an assembly line but which did not work.

In some factories expensive machines were available but there was a shortage of nails and bricks. These had previously been produced by groups of peasants and their production had been disrupted by collectivisation. For the same reason there was a shortage of animals needed to pull carts and waggons.

Shortage of trained workers

There was a shortage of workers to be employed in the new industrial enterprises. This was met by the massive shift of population caused by collectivisation. Millions of people moved from the countryside to the new industrial enterprises. Most lacked even a basic education and few had the technical skills needed to work the new machines. This led to the breakage of machines and a high rate of industrial accidents. John Scott, an American engineer who worked in the USSR commented "I would wager that Russia's battle of ferrous metallurgy alone involved more casualties than the battle of the Marne" (*Behind the Urals*, 1942).

Lack of worker discipline

The new workers were not used to the discipline needed in modern industries. Workers were often late, or they drifted from job to job. The state took severe measures to try to stop this behaviour. In 1932 one day off work without a good reason could lead to instant dismissal with loss of home and ration card. By 1939 'absenteeism' was defined as being 20 minutes late. In 1940 it could be punished by a 25% pay cut for six months. By this date prison was used to punish any worker who left a job without permission. As early as 1932 the death penalty was used to punish theft of state property and internal passports had been introduced to restrict movement.

The fact that the state introduced such penalties illustrates the extent of the problems faced. The fact that the penalties increased in severity indicates the weakness of the state and its failure to halt the problems. As late as 1938 the average Soviet worker changed jobs every 17 months.

Attempts were made to reward good workers with better pay, pensions, housing and awards. This culminated in the Stakhanovite movement, which started in September 1935. It was named after a miner – Aleksei Stakhanov from the Donbass coalfield – who on one shift dug 14 times the amount of coal expected. His output was assisted by helpers and equipment which worked, but his achievement became nationally famous and was used to encourage other workers to emulate his massive productivity. While some workers resented the privileges of Stakhanovites and the pressure they put on others to copy them, recent research suggests that many workers put pressure on their managers to let them become Stakhanovites. The success of the movement indicates that a significant number of workers were highly motivated by it.

Workers formed 'Shock Brigades' and attempted impossible targets under slogans such as 'There are no fortresses which Bolsheviks cannot conquer'.

The Five-Year Plans: success or failure?

The Five-Year Plans have, with some justification been called 'Stalin's Revolution'. They transformed the USSR and rank amongst the most astonishing achievements in 20th-century history. Yet their achievements were mixed.

The growth of industrial production

Historians such as Robert Service have suggested that the NEP had the potential to support industrialisation and that it had already laid important foundations but that Stalin "ignored the progress made in the later imperial and early Soviet epochs" (*The Russian Revolution* 1900–27, 1991). However, even allowing for this, the leap in output after 1929 was enormous and the growth of industrial enterprises staggering.

Some 1,500 huge power stations, factories and metal-working complexes were built during the First Five-Year Plan. These included the vast steel production centre at Magnitogorsk, tractor factories at Cheliabinsk and Stalingrad, automobile factories in Moscow and Sormovo to name but a few. Existing industries expanded dramatically and new ones were established such as the production of machine-tools, aircraft and synthetic rubber. Production figures soared (see Appendix 3). Thousands of miles of railways and canals were built. The number of workers doubled between 1928 and 1932 alone.

The distribution of industry

A feature of the Five-Year Plans was the creation of industries in areas that had not previously been industrialised. This affected areas as far apart as Byelorussia in the west and Siberia and Buriat-Mongolia in the Far East. When the Germans overran large areas of the western USSR in 1941–42, it was these new industries east of the Urals which made the Soviet counterattack and eventual victory possible. This must count as one of the most important achievements of the Five-Year Plans.

A new mood in the country

Social

The Five-Year Plans clearly succeeded in harnessing the enthusiasm of many citizens, especially the young. This has to be seen as one of its achievements, to be set alongside the raw figures of industrial production. The Stakhanovite movement is an example of this phenomenon though even this, it must be added had complex effects.

On one hand it motivated many workers and by rewarding them harnessed support for the regime and its aims. It also allowed these workers the privileged position to speak out concerning working conditions. Many also used their position to criticise managers who they considered were unsympathetic to the needs of workers. This goes a long way towards answering the assumption that Soviet workers were the victims of the Five-Year Plans. Clearly many benefited from them and used these benefits as a means by which their views could be expressed and so "felt greater legitimacy for the political system because their views were being so widely solicited" (R. Thurston, *Life and Terror in Stalin's Russia*, 1996).

working conditions

On the other hand Stakhanovites caused tensions within industries as their drive to exceed their targets could disrupt the organisation of an enterprise. Also there is evidence of Stakhanovites tinkering with machines to improve output, but damaging them due to lack of expertise. Managers grew afraid of ignoring Stakhanovite demands. The Director of the Gorkii Auto Factory in 1935 estimated he spent 15–30% of his time having to organise Stakhanovites. Consequently the movement had both negative as well as positive effects.

Weaknesses of the Five-Year Plans

economic

On the negative side the Plans frequently failed to meet their targets. However, since these targets were set more for effect than achievability, this shortcoming should not be taken too seriously, as the increase in production by 1941 was vast.

Nevertheless, questions need to be asked about the reliability of some of the achievement figures. The pressure to meet targets was enormous and production figures were often falsified. Added to this the state manipulated the statistics to make them sound more impressive, for example using 1926–27 prices for goods not made in these years.

More fundamental are reservations about the actual industrial base that was created. By the end of the First Five-Year Plan it was clear that worker productivity was very low and remained disappointing thereafter. Most of the achievements by 1933 had come simply from using existing resources more efficiently. The Second Five-Year Plan set more realistic targets and over-fulfilled them by 3% on average. Its achievements were made possible by the fact that new plants, built during the First Five-Year Plan, entered production. However, in a number of areas (e.g. oil and textiles) output was disappointing. The achievements in heavy industry were not matched across the economy. Nor were problems in transportation – vital in so large a country – fully overcome. An obsession with quantity over quality caused many products to be shoddy and unreliable and meant that many Soviet goods did not compare well with Western ones. The Third Five-Year Plan continued the focus on heavy industry but also increased defence expenditure. Its achievements are harder to assess as it was cut short in 1941 by the Nazi invasion.

Social

To these problems should be added the human cost. Lives were lost in

Social.

pursuing targets as if the cost was of little consequence. Living conditions [*Social.*] were poor and consumer goods scarce. Like the prevalence of poor quality goods, the lack of consumer goods has continued to dog Soviet and post-Soviet society – a legacy of the nature of Stalin's Five-Year Plans.

Planned economy, or organised chaos?

The organisation of the Five-Year Plans was overseen by a state agency, Gosplan. In theory Gosplan set the targets which were to be met by specific industries. However, this gives it a scientific character which often failed to develop in reality. For example, during the First Five-Year Plan Stalin increased some of its targets by over 100%. Such adjustments made a non-sense of planning and were done for political effect. [*Gosplan → Political.*]

More significantly, Gosplan set general targets; it was up to managers on the ground to translate these into specific action plans. This meant that the decisions of the State Planning Commission – already often unrealistic and arbitrary – rapidly degenerated into desperate and confused strategies to [*Social.*] meet these demands at the level of an individual factory, or mine. Consequently the system was often cumbersome and inflexible and, at the same time, chaotic and poorly planned. Despite the claim to be a 'planned economy' many targets were only achieved by "intrigue and string pulling" (A. Nove, An *Economic History of the* USSR, 1989).

Paradoxically the greatest stimulus to increased state control came from the massive problems faced in implementing the plans. Each new crisis and bottleneck increased the tendency to, in Moshe Lewin's phrase,"close loopholes by putting the hand on more levers" (R*ussia/USSR/Russia*,1995).

Success or failure?

The official Soviet statistics of the 1930s do not reveal the full picture regarding the achievements of the Five-Year Plans. The whole process was much more confused and mixed than they suggest. Alongside the transformation must be set the shortages, the waste, the confusion and the human cost. Nevertheless, as the more realistic targets of the Second Five-Year Plan reveal, Stalin's government was capable of learning from its errors and revising its goals. Consequently, though the areas of weakness were significant the overall achievement was considerable. The Five-Year Plans can, with some justification, be termed 'Stalin's Revolution'.

Studying 'The Five-Year Plans'

1   Carefully study the figures for industrial production shown in Appendix 3.
     a) What do these show you about the strength and weakness of the Five-Year Plans?
     b) What other data would you need,other than that given in the Appendix, in order to decide whether the Five-Year Plans were a success, or not?

2   Using Appendix 3, the map of industrial locations opposite and the other information in this section, how accurate is it to suggest that Stalin takes the credit for a 'Second Revolution' which transformed the USSR?

Figure 3
The distribution of industry in the USSR as a result of the Five-Year Plans.

4 The Terror

Strong state versus weak society, or weak state in crisis?

Key points

◆ Was the Terror a new departure or a continuation of established policy?
◆ Do the purges of the 1930s follow a clear pattern of development?
◆ The murder of Kirov
◆ Causes of the Great Terror?
◆ To what extent did the Terror damage the USSR?

The Terror: a new departure, or a continuation of established policy?

During the mid- to late 1930s the USSR experienced a mounting Terror; the secret police were responsible for arresting, imprisoning and executing huge numbers of Soviet citizens. The word 'Terror' implies the indiscriminate use of force against a population. In such a process people are accused of imagined, or trivial crimes. Their imprisonment, or death, is not due to their guilt but instead to a deliberate attempt by the government to control society through the use of fear. To what extent this was true of the USSR in the 1930s is the subject of critical enquiry by historians.

Was there Terror before the 1930s?

An important question is whether Stalin was responsible for a new policy in the USSR, or whether there was already an established tradition of Terror? Aleksandr Solzhenitsyn (in *The Gulag Archipelago*, 1974) insisted that there was a tradition of Terror dating to the Bolshevik seizure of power and that Stalin escalated a tendency that had always existed in Bolshevik rule. He pointed to the killing of hostages and other atrocities during the Civil War and the banning of other political parties in the 1920s. These acts predated Stalin's collectivisation of agriculture after 1928, and the show trial of engineers accused of wrecking coal mines in the Shakhty Trial of 1928, which itself pre-dated the mass arrests of the 1930s.

In short, Solzhenitsyn argued that the Communists seized power without popular support and consistently used fear and violence to keep in power. This was a process started by Lenin and continued by Stalin in the late 1920s and escalated by him during the 1930s.

While there is some truth in this view there are also significant differences between the use of Terror in the 1930s and previous uses:

◆ Terror in the Civil War had occurred under exceptional circumstances, when Communist rule was under threat. That of the mid- to late 1930s took place when Communist rule was firmly in place.

◆ There is evidence that before he died Lenin was concerned at the illegal use of violence in the USSR when it victimised Party members and workers.

◆ Terror in the 1920s was usually applied to obvious opponents of the Party. Terror in the mid- to late 1930s fell heavily on the Party itself and on people who had committed no 'crimes' of opposition.

◆ The scale of imprisonment and executions in Terror before 1928 was much less than in later uses of Terror.

Consequently, while Terror had been used by the Party before 1928 there were significant differences between it and what occurred after 1928 and especially the Terror in the 1930s. Nevertheless, Lenin set a precedent of violence.

The pattern of the purges

During the 1930s Stalin's government carried out a number of attempts to remove people from positions of power who were regarded as a threat, as traitors, or incompetent. These actions culminated in the mass arrests which occurred in the mid- to late 1930s.

It is quite common to describe all the attempts by Stalin's government to remove undesirable people as 'purges'. However, this is wrong. The Russian word for purge (*chistka* – meaning cleaning out) should only be applied to the attempts to clean-up the Party by removing people who were thought unworthy of being Party members. These purges did not involve the arrest or execution of the people expelled from the Party. Nor were such purges of the Party new. Similar purges had occurred in 1919, 1921, 1924, 1925, 1928 and 1929. They were attempts to ensure that Party members were dedicated and active. Any who did little, or were accused of moral weaknesses, or who came from 'unreliable' social origins (e.g. middle-class, kulaks, ex-White army officers, etc.) were to be removed.

Figure 4
The pattern of the purges in the 1930s.

1933	Purge of Party	Expulsion of 'alien', 'unreliable' and 'disreputable' elements from the Party.
1935	Verification of Party Documents	Sorting out of chaotic Party membership records and expulsion of people seen as undesirable, or who had gained Party membership through illegal means.
1936	Exchange of Party Documents	Due to the failure of the Verification of Party Documents campaign, new Party cards issued and expulsion of undesirable Party members.
1937–38	The Ezhovshchina ('time of Ezhov')	Mass arrests of Party members, ex-oppositionists, military and non-Party members. The 'Terror' was named after Ezhov, commander of the secret police from 1936.

These purges were not uses of Terror, nor did they apply to non-Party members. They were very different from the mass arrests and executions which occurred after 1937. They cannot be seen as representing a pattern of increasing violence, although they are often referred to as if they were part of one process in which Stalin's government destroyed all potential opposition.

The one sense in which they do suggest a pattern of development is that they indicate the weakness of Stalin's government immediately preceding the Terror of 1937–38. All of the purges arose from the government's frustration with the way the Party was organised. It was clear that membership records were in a mess and that undesirable people had got into the Party in order to protect themselves, or advance their ambitions. Each of the purges failed to remedy this situation. To the Party leadership the reason for this failure was clear – local Party bosses (secretaries) refused to reform the Party. Such bosses looked after their own allies and purged innocent Party members, instead of responding to central government directives to improve Party efficiency. By 1936 there is strong evidence to suggest that the central leadership of the Party was determined to destroy the power of these local Party secretaries.

The purges of 1933–36, far from demonstrating the power of Stalin and his allies, revealed their inability to control and govern the Party. Such a sense of weakness encouraged radical solutions to remedy the 'problem'.

Who killed Kirov?

In December 1934 Sergei Kirov, the boss of the Leningrad Party was shot dead by a lone assassin, Leonid Nikolaev. His death shocked the Party and its leadership.

To some of them it seemed to indicate the existence of anti-Communist terrorist organisations in the USSR. In 1953 the secret police defector, Alexander Orlov, alleged that Stalin had organised the killing. In so doing he had removed a rival for power and provided himself with the excuse for unleashing Terror on the USSR in order to destroy old enemies and any potential opposition to his rule.

The case against Stalin

◆ Kirov was a popular Party leader and a potential rival to Stalin. In 1956 the defector, Nicolaevsky, suggested that Kirov was planning reforms which would have reduced Stalin's power and that of the police, given increased rights to collective farmers and increased democracy generally.

◆ Stalin used the murder as a reason to rush through the 'Law of 1 December 1934', giving the secret police the power to speed up the process of executing people accused of terrorism. The 'guilty' were not allowed to appeal and could be swiftly shot.

◆ On 16 December 1934 Zinoviev, Kamenev and 13 of their allies – all people who had earlier opposed Stalin – were arrested. The press hinted at links between them and Kirov's death. In the later Show Trials, after 1936, oppositionists were accused of complicity in Kirov's murder.

The case for Stalin's defence

◆ No-one before 1953 accused Stalin. The accusation coincided with the growing Cold War of the 1950s.

◆ Khrushchev, Soviet leader in the 1950s, accused Stalin of being responsible for the deaths of many Party members but made no accusation about Kirov.

◆ There is no clear evidence of a dispute between Kirov and Stalin, despite suggestions that Kirov polled more votes than Stalin in the 1934 elections to the Central Committee. Kirov was no moderate and did not offer a radically different alternative to Stalin. In 1937 Trotsky described Kirov as "Leningrad dictator" and other oppositionists also thought he was a hardliner.

◆ The secret police seem implicated: they failed to protect Kirov, they had previously detained then released the assassin. However, there is no evidence that Stalin ordered this. In fact Kirov's bodyguard died in a mysterious accident before he could be questioned by Stalin.

◆ The assassin had no links with opposition groups. His diary insisted he was acting alone. If Stalin intended to use the killing as an excuse to attack oppositionists, a link with opposition groups could easily have been concocted; it was not.

◆ The 'Law of 1 December 1934' was rarely used. Instead, the government response to Kirov's murder was chaotic. They did not know who to blame. Although Zinoviev and Kamenev were arrested, no link was made with the actual killing until later and the mass arrest of oppositionists did not occur until mid-1936.

The significance of Kirov's murder

The case against Stalin is far from proven. Indeed, the immediate reaction of Stalin and his allies was not a calculated use of the killing to further their own ambitions but instead "confusion and mindless, unfocussed rage" (J. Arch Getty, *Origins of the Great Purges*, 1985).

The evidence does not suggest that Stalin stage-managed the progression towards Terror. In fact in 1933 Stalin had ordered the release of half of all labour camp prisoners and in the summer of 1934 had ordered that the secret police could not carry out executions without the agreement of the procurator of the USSR. These were hardly the actions of a man gearing himself up for a massive attack on society and planning Kirov's death as the trigger for that attack.

As with so much in the history of Stalin's USSR the reality seems more chaotic and muddled than is sometimes presented. Later, Stalin was prepared to use the Kirov murder as part of his excuse for destroying members of ex-opposition groups. But the evidence suggests that, while this was useful to him, there is no definite proof that he ordered the murder, or initially reacted to it in a calculated manner.

What caused the Great Terror?

In 1936 Stalin alleged that the secret police were four years behind in the unmasking of oppositionists working against the government of the USSR. This may have been a reference to a plot against him, discovered in 1932 and led by a Party leader named Riutin. Stalin had not forgotten the threat. In August 1936 the first of the great show trials began. It involved Zinoviev, Kamenev and their allies. They confessed to being responsible for attempts to wreck Soviet industry and kill Soviet leaders. They were found guilty and shot.

In January 1937 at the trial of the one-time Trotskyist, Piatakov, evidence was presented which incriminated Bukharin and his allies Rykov and Tomsky. Tomsky had committed suicide in August 1936. In July 1937 high-ranking military officers were shot, on charges of treason. An unparalleled Terror swept through the country. Vast camp complexes were set up in the most inhospitable regions of the USSR. Prisoners who escaped execution were used as slave labour on various projects and worked to death. Eventually, in March 1938, Bukharin and members of the old Right Deviation were brought to trial. Like the previous defendants they were accused of working with the exiled Trotsky and foreign governments against the USSR. All confessed and were shot.

The question remains however as to how much this Terror was initiated by Stalin as a deliberate 'tool' of his government; a conscious plan on his part. A number of factors lay behind the beginning of a policy of Terror in 1937. These factors are varied and suggest Stalin's motivation and his responsibility for the policy may be equally complex.

The personal ambition of Stalin

The classic explanation for the Terror is that Stalin used it to:

a.   Destroy anyone who had ever opposed him.
b.   Destroy anyone who had the potential to oppose him.
c.   So terrify and disorientate the population that it was impossible for any opposition to his rule to be organised.

Nadezhda Mandelstam expressed the view that the function of the Terror was "To plunge the whole country into a state of chronic fear" and that this was a conscious policy chosen by Stalin, following a pattern by which "waves of terror recurred from time to time" (*Hope Against Hope*, 1971). Many traditional interpretations agree with Mandelstam's. Roy Medvedev stated that the roots of the Terror lay in "Stalin's inordinate vanity and lust for power" (*On Stalin and Stalinism*, 1979) and Robert Conquest believed the reason lay in the desire "to destroy or disorganise all possible sources of opposition to Stalin's progress to absolute rule" (*The Great Terror: A Reassessment*, 1990).

The initial targets for the Terror, according to such analyses, were the Old Bolsheviks; those long-term Party members with independent minds, who did not owe their position to Stalin. Their destruction allowed Stalin to bring in a new class of government and Party officials who were totally obedient to him.

The war scare

The rise of Fascism and the growing threat from Germany caused alarm in the USSR. The show trials coincided with Nazi expansion in the Rhineland, Austria and Czechoslovakia. A genuine fear of impending war may have caused the Soviet leadership to think it necessary to remove any leaders capable of criticising Stalin's handling of foreign policy or conduct of a war, if it occurred. Coupled with this was a genuine fear of counter-revolutionary spies in the pay of enemy countries.

There may even have been a possibility that the military leaders – such as Marshal Tukhachevsky, accused of treason in June 1937 – really were planning a coup against Stalin. So, Terror might have arisen out of a genuine, though brutal, desire to protect the Revolution not simply to enhance Stalin's personal power.

Internal Party rivalries

Serious differences existed amongst the leadership of the USSR over the direction in which industry and society should develop. These differences were made more bitter by the need to remedy massive problems associated with the implementation of the Five-Year Plans.

Ordzhonikidze, commissar for heavy industry since 1932, believed that industrial targets should be realistic. He resisted attempts by the secret police to make factory managers the scapegoats for problems in the economy; a process that had escalated in the spring of 1936.

Set against him were more radical leaders who wanted faster change. Amongst these was Ezhov, the chairman of the Party's Control Commission, responsible for ensuring that government decisions were carried out. He believed that problems were the result of class enemies deliberately trying to 'wreck' the USSR. He was supported by Molotov, chairman of Sovnarkom (the government of the USSR) and a loyal supporter of Stalin.

Stalin appears not to have committed himself consistently to any of these alternative approaches. In 1934 he backed the moderates and more realistic targets for the Second Five-Year Plan. In 1936 he shifted his position and backed the radicals. This was probably encouraged by concerns that the Stakhanovite movement was being obstructed by industrial managers and the demands of the radicals that the secret police should be let loose on these 'wreckers'.

The arrest of Piatakov was an attack by Ezhov and Molotov on Ordzhonikidze, since Piatakov was his deputy. The weakness of Piatakov was that he had once been a Trotskyist. His arrest signalled that Stalin had thrown his weight behind the radicals. In September 1936, three days after explosions at the Siberian Kemerovo coal mines, Iagoda, head of the secret police, was replaced by the more radical Ezhov. In November 1936 managers of the Kemerovo Pits were accused of sabotaging the mines there in the so-called Novosibirsk Trial. The secret police were about to be let loose to hunt out so called 'enemies of the people'. In January 1937 Piatakov was shot; shortly afterwards Ordzhonikidze committed suicide.

Centre versus the regions

The purges of the early 1930s revealed that Stalin and the Moscow-based leaders of the Party were unable to make local Party bosses obey them. Time and again these regional Party secretaries ignored instructions from the leadership, or failed to tackle the corruption and chaos in the Party organisation.

Such local Party bosses often had close relationships with local military leaders, many of whom had been denounced as traitors after June 1937.

One interpretation of the Terror is that it was a radical measure by a weak state desperate to find a way to destroy regional leaders who were ignoring its commands. From February 1937 the aim of Stalin's central government was to "unleash criticism of the middle-level *apparat* [Party secretaries] by the rank and file activists" (J. Arch Getty, *Origins of the Great Purges*, 1985).

This tactic released a pent-up surge of discontent and anger felt by ordinary Party members. It was an opportunity to hold local Party leaders responsible for all social and economic failures. Recent research has shown that it was not Old Bolsheviks who were targeted but those holding middle-ranking Party and government posts. Some were Old Bolsheviks; many were not.

The Terror was also an opportunity for ordinary Party members to settle old scores, give release to envy and seek promotion by destroying rivals. Once started, the process rapidly got out of control. What had begun as a blood-letting within the Party soon engulfed the nation in two years of increasing chaos and paranoia. Such a Terror then arose from a contradictory process established by the Five-Year Plans – "the erection of a superbureaucratic state and simultaneously antibureaucratic fury" (M. Lewin, *Russia/USSR/Russia*, 1995).

Stalin – a man with a plan?

The evidence suggests that for much of the 1930s Stalin held the middle ground amongst his competing colleagues in the run-up to the Ezhovshchina. Stalin does not appear to have followed one consistent policy leading from collectivisation to the Terror.

Destroying his political rivals was clearly one of the motives behind the Terror but it would be wrong to see the Terror as arising solely from Stalin's ambitions. There appear to have been genuine anxieties in the Party leadership about failures in the economy, foreign espionage, class-enemies and about the inability of central government to impose its will on the regional Party bosses. It was this basic weakness – coupled with pressure by Party leaders such as Ezhov to use secret police powers to remove bureaucrats who were stifling Revolutionary enthusiasm – that led to the chaotic explosion of violence in 1937–38. The final 'trigger' appears to have been Ezhov's claim that the secret police had uncovered evidence of a military plot. When the Terror erupted it met both popular support as well as horror; its energy came from 'below' as much as from 'above' and it was this that gave it its particular character. In this it had similarities with Lenin's use of Terror, which had also harnessed existing hatreds and which had partly "erupted from below" (O. Figes, *A People's Tragedy*, 1996). These complex factors suggest that to sum up the Terror as "the thriller Stalin was concocting" (E. Radzinsky, *Stalin*, 1996) is rather too simplistic, as it suggests he totally controlled it and its direction.

Nevertheless, whilst Stalin did not single-handedly plan a policy of Terror, he must take responsibility for turning a tense atmosphere into massive violence. It was Stalin who reopened the investigation into Kirov's murder in early 1936 (implying a plot lay behind it); Stalin allowed the condemnation of Piatakov; in June 1937 Stalin backed Ezhov and his widespread secret police hunt for 'wreckers'. He encouraged the idea that 'wreckers' were infiltrating the USSR. At the 1937 plenum of the Central Committee he asserted: "while there is capitalist encirclement there will be sabotage, terrorism, diversions and spies." Talk like this fuelled the Terror.

Stalin's cold-blooded willingness to destroy other people can be seen in a letter written to his chief supporter Molotov as early as August 1930. With regard to government financial problems he casually suggested "shoot two or three dozen wreckers, including several dozen common cashiers" (quoted in L. T. Lih *et al.*, S*talin's Letters to Molotov*, 1995). The recently opened Presidential Archives show Stalin's signature on 366 death sentence lists, totalling 44,000 people, in 1938 alone. When one Old Bolshevik – Yakir – wrote Stalin a letter, shortly before his execution, stating his love for his leader, Stalin simply added the comment "villain and prostitute. Stalin." Kaganovich, one of his deputies added the remark "scum, bastard, whore". Such newly available documents reveal the coarse brutality and cruelty encouraged by Stalin and his closest colleagues.

However, although Stalin's brutality and vindictiveness was appalling, his rule was not simply one of escalating violence. When the Ezhovshchina began to run out of control in 1938 he sacrificed Ezhov in order to signal a change of direction. Ezhov was removed from his post as head of the secret police in May 1938. In the spring of 1939 he was arrested. (Recently discovered documents suggest he was shot in February 1940.) The activities of the secret police were then more tightly controlled. Party activists and workers were no longer encouraged to denounce their local leaders and managers. Though the USSR continued to suffer brutal police repression the Great Terror – the Ezhovshchina – was over.

To what extent did the Terror hurt the USSR?

Ferocious debates still continue amongst historians concerning the number of Stalin's victims. The Russian historian Roy Medvedev suggested 5–7 million people were repressed in 1937–38 alone. Another Russian writer, Shatunovskaia, suggested that between 1935 and 1941 almost 20 million people were arrested, of whom 7 million were shot. In the West, Robert Conquest estimated that the camp population in 1939 numbered 9 million. However these figures now appear to be far too high. Work since 1991 in Russia, by the historian Zemskov and based on recently released secret police archives, suggests a much lower camp population (see Appendix 4). Alec Nove has suggested that the number of deaths related to the Terror may have been in the region of three million. Of these, recent work in Russia, in 1992, by V. Popov suggests over 600,000 were shot in 1937–38.

The Terror was not uniform, hitting some areas, Party organisations and factories more than others. Work in the USA (at the Project on the Soviet Social System, Harvard University) based on personal recollections of the Terror suggests a significant number of ordinary people did not feel under threat.

Impact of the Terror

Even the lower casualty figures draw attention to the tremendous damage done to the USSR by the Terror. Large numbers of government and Party officials died, along with managers in industry. Administration was disrupted and the loss of skills and expertise caused chaos in planning and in industrial production. Terror led to the stifling of creative discussion over how to solve the problems of the USSR.

With regard to the military, the Terror broke (in Moshe Lewin's phrase) its "backbone and brain" (*Russia/USSR/Russia*, 1995). Whilst older estimates of the number of officers arrested failed to take into account the large number reinstated after 1939 and overestimated the size of the officer corps, still some 22,700 officers were killed, imprisoned, or expelled from the military (R. Reese, 'The Red Army and the Great Purges', in *Stalinist Terror, New Perspectives*, 1993). This left the Soviet military weakened in the face of Hitler's attack on the USSR in 1941.

However, this weakness should not be over exaggerated. In 1941 there was still great loyalty to the regime and Soviet soldiers resisted the German advance with great courage. As Robert Thurston has pointed out, 1941 was the "Acid Test" for Stalin's regime and the fact that it survived suggests that, surprisingly, the Terror was not responsible for the depth of demoralisation and chaos that is sometimes suggested (*Life and Terror in Stalin's Russia*, 1996). The Soviet people were tremendously resilient despite the sufferings of the 1930s.

Studying 'The Terror'

1 Many traditional interpretations of the Terror focus only on Stalin. However, our understanding of this period of Soviet history can be assisted by looking at the parts played by other individuals. Make notes (a short paragraph for each) on the role in the 1930s of the following Party leaders. Indicate the contribution they made to the emergence of the Terror:
  ◆ Ezhov,
  ◆ Molotov,
  ◆ Iagoda,
  ◆ Ordzhonikidze.

2 The killing of Kirov is one of the central events in many accounts of the origins of the Terror. From what you have read in this chapter ,and from other research, what do you think is the most convincing explanation of who was responsible for Kirov's murder?

3 In order to gain an impression of what life was like in the Stalinist Gulag read *One Day in the Life of Ivan Denisovich*, by Solzhenitsyn.

Figure 5

The distribution of camps (the Gulag) administered by the secret police as a result of the Terror.

Legend:
- Region set aside for completely isolated camps
- Region set aside for forced labour
- Main forced labour camps

Map labels:

1,000 km

JAPAN

Vladivostok

Magadan

Kolyma labour camps

Yakutsk

Siberia

Lake Baikal

Irkutsk

MONGOLIA

CHINA

Arctic Ocean

UNION OF SOVIET SOCIALIST REPUBLICS

Ural Mts

Central Asia

FINLAND

Leningrad

Moscow

Kiev

Ukraine

Stalingrad

Caspian Sea

Baku

IRAN

POLAND

Odessa

Black Sea

5 Was Soviet society transformed under Stalin?

Social policy, cultural policy and religion

Key points

◆ Why was there a Cultural Revolution 1929–32?
◆ Did Stalin's government have a consistent policy on women and the family?
◆ The impact of the state on religion
◆ The impact of the state on the creative arts

Why was there a Cultural Revolution?

During the First Five-Year Plan (1929–33) Soviet society was shaken and challenged by an experience sometimes described as a 'Cultural Revolution'. Tremendous social changes mirrored the enormous economic changes which were a feature of rapid industrialisation.

Characteristics of the Cultural Revolution

◆ Continued emphasis on recruitment of new workers into the Party. An enrolment in 1927 followed the campaigns of the Lenin Enrolment of 1924–25.

◆ Workers were encouraged to criticise non-Party managers and specialists (*spetsy*) in industry.

◆ Campaigns encouraged younger workers into higher education, especially in fields relevant to industrial growth such as engineering.

◆ The state persecuted non-Party managers who were held to be actively responsible for industrial failures and accidents. The most notable example of this was the Shakhty Trial, 1928.

Factors behind the upheaval

The Cultural Revolution can be seen as a process stimulated by Stalin's political ambitions. The replacement of managers with a new generation of young working-class men and women was both a popular move amongst Party members and workers and meant that the new generation of the élite were dependent on Stalin. The move also undermined criticism made by the Left and United Oppositions that the Party leadership was out of touch with rank and file workers and Party members. At the same time attacks on those managers and economists who had reservations about the impossible targets set by the Five-Year Plan swept away opposition to Stalin's 'Second Revolution'.

However, while there is some truth in this interpretation it is too simplistic a view. It is clear that "Cultural revolution involved a response on behalf of the leadership to pressures within the Communist movement and society as a whole" (S. Fitzpatrick, *Cultural Revolution in Russia*, 1978). Working-class frustration with the NEP was genuine. A desire for workers to be more influential and upwardly mobile had been growing throughout the 1920s. Cultural Revolution was both exciting and opened up opportunities to exercise power and influence hitherto denied to many workers. Whilst the Party undoubtedly stirred up this revolution in some areas, in others young Communist intellectuals spontaneously set the process in motion once Stalin's government ceased to protect the NEP and encouraged dramatic industrial and social change.

A policy of 'rudeness'?

Lenin, in an addition made to his 'Testament' in January 1923, had condemned Stalin as "too rude, a fault tolerable in the relations among us Communists, which becomes intolerable in the office of General Secretary". However, during the Cultural Revolution Stalin was to turn such a character to his distinct advantage. His frequent open admissions of being "blunt and rude" were not intended as confessions of weakness. Instead he was aligning himself with a new mood of impatience in the Party, which expressed itself in working-class attacks on specialists and intolerance of moderate opinions. The fact that the General Secretary identified himself with such a mood had the clear effect of "declaring the legitimacy of such an outlook" (L. Siegelbaum, *Soviet State and Society Between Revolutions*, 1918–29, 1992).

In this sense the Cultural Revolution allowed Stalin to make a virtue out of his own leadership style and gave him the opportunity to harness mass Party support. It was a similar appeal to the Party rank and file which in 1937 lay behind the explosion of violence of the Ezhovshchina. In neither case did Stalin create the mood. However, he had the political skill to legitimise and release these emotions in such a way as to benefit from them and use their force to sweep away opposition to his policies. This was the feature of much of his leadership. Far from being the totalitarian puppet-master dominating Soviet society, he was more of a political surfer who knew how to recognise and ride the waves of social tension which he had sometimes encouraged but not created.

The end of the Cultural Revolution

By the end of the First Five-Year Plan the Cultural Revolution had both achieved its objectives and had begun to undermine the orderly running of industry. From 1932 the state began to discourage the disorderly specialist baiting and egalitarian features, such as equality of pay, associated with the Cultural Revolution. A new orderliness was ushered in with the Second Five-Year Plan. Workers experienced increased discipline; managers and skilled workers – many of whom had risen to their positions since 1929 – were rewarded with better pay and conditions than other less qualified workers. The turmoil of the Cultural Revolution was over.

Education

The Cultural Revolution had caused upheaval in education. Young Communists (the 'Komsomol') attacked middle-class students and teachers; many teachers lost their jobs. Traditional schooling gave way to social and political work, and formal tests were replaced by students assessing their own progress. The result was poorly disciplined children, whose education was heavily politicised but lacking in the basic skills required by the industries of the Five-Year Plans.

In 1931 the Central Committee ordered a shift back to more traditional education. A core curriculum was introduced and was assessed by formal tests. By 1939 school uniforms had returned, along with fees for advanced secondary education and compulsory pigtails for girls!

Did Stalin's government have a consistent policy on women and the family?

Attitudes towards women and the family had undergone great changes during the 1920s. A women's department of the Central Committee – Zhenotdel – had been set up in 1919 and had encouraged free abortion, easier divorce laws, female literacy and the growth in the number of women workers. Civil marriage had been recognised, as part of the Communist state's opposition to the church and its influence. The 1926 Law Code extended property rights to women living with their partners.

These changes had a number of functions. Increased female emancipation was clearly one, but the state also undermined the institution of the family. This was regarded as a bourgeois creation.

The situation inherited by Stalin

By the time Stalin came to power in the late 1920s, this policy had already suffered setbacks. During the NEP state assistance to women and children, in the form of health and welfare assistance, had been cut back. State support for abortion had also been reduced. The state's previous policies had met resistance in many areas. Many male Party members had been less than enthusiastic about the activities of the Zhenotdel and it had faced fierce resistance in rural areas, particularly in Muslim ones. The attempt to increase the role of women within the Party had had only limited success. By 1930 only 13.5% of Party members were women.

The policies of Stalin's government

In 1930 the Zhenotdel was closed as it was considered to have fulfilled its aims. This action of course illustrates the lack of support for its activities within the Party hierarchy and amongst many ordinary Party workers.

The official attitude towards women and the family during the 1930s was contradictory. Officially women had the same opportunities as men and the 'Woman Question', as it had been termed in the 1920s, had been declared 'solved'. In reality policy was more complex.

Women were still encouraged to work and from 1928 to 1940 the number of female workers rose from 3 to 13 million. This growth in the number of women workers was a tremendous social change and accompanied the expansion of industry of the Five-Year Plans. However, many women were still employed in traditionally 'female jobs', such as in the textile industry and they were poorly represented in heavy industries such as steel-making, construction and engineering. Women also continued to experience lower rates of pay than men and were less likely to be promoted.

In terms of general policy towards family life a distinctly traditional view reasserted itself against the changes encouraged in the early 1920s. A combination of the upheaval caused by collectivisation and relaxed sexual relations had led to a breakdown in family life in many parts of the USSR. Gangs of orphan and unwanted children became a major problem in many cities. Some became beggars, others thieves who were often highly organised and violent. These problems led to an adoption of policies designed to preserve family life: abortion was restricted as was contraception and access to divorce. In 1935 the official view was expressed as: "The state cannot exist without the family."

It is clear then that, despite the encouragement of women to work, Stalin's government adopted an increasingly traditional approach to both the role of women and the family. In many ways this was consistent with trends emerging by the late 1920s and the policies of the 1930s were less a sudden return to traditional values and more an acceleration of existing trends.

What was the impact of the state on religion?

The Communist Party was committed to the destruction of religious belief. Until the need to unite all sections of the population against German invasion in 1941, religious believers suffered frequent persecution. That outright destruction was not attempted was largely due to the widespread support for the Russian Orthodox Church, especially in the countryside. Islam was strongly supported in many of the south/central Asian republics and there were many Jews, especially in western Russia.

During the Civil War atrocities against priests and the destruction of religious buildings had been widespread. The NEP saw a reduction in these attacks but the state still put considerable energy into encouraging divisions within the leadership of the Orthodox Church and arresting priests and bishops who were not submissive to the state.

A new law in 1929 made it illegal to engage in religious activity outside of church buildings and only officially licensed congregations were allowed to meet for worship.

Collectivisation saw a renewal of violent attacks on churches, priests and active believers. The same happened to Muslims (who for a brief period in the early 1920s, had experienced less state persecution), Islamic law was banned and women were encouraged to unveil. Prayer and fasting was openly condemned and in 1935 the pilgrimage to Mecca was prohibited. Jews initially received a respite from the kind of persecution experienced under the Tsars but faced anti-Semitism amongst Party leaders and during the 1930s suffered the same pressures as other religious believers.

Many religious believers fell victim to the Terror. By 1939 only 12 out of the 163 bishops active in 1930 had escaped arrest and imprisonment. This was despite efforts by many in a leadership position to give concessions to the regime.

Despite these pressures religious believers did not disappear. Whilst a significant number probably did drift away, or compromised, many others met in secret. Orthodox believers who resisted state control looked for leadership to the imprisoned Metropolitan Josif of Leningrad. Other Christian groups, such as Baptists who had suffered persecution under the Tsars, also met secretly in homes and out of doors. In the northern Caucasus and in Central Asia there were outbreaks of Islamic resistance and many Muslims met in secret.

Soviet anti-religious policy – though more consistent than some other Soviet social policies – demonstrates the limitations facing even the most authoritarian state. Years of persecution failed to destroy religious belief. In 1941 Stalin reversed the policy of persecuting religious believers when the German invasion forced him to take measures to unite Russian society around traditional Russian values.

What was the impact of the state on the creative arts?

Many artists viewed the 1917 Revolution as a liberating force. The Communist Party was eager to exploit the educative and propaganda opportunities presented by the creative arts. The 1920s saw an explosion of experimental artistic creativity in art, design, music and literature.

However, the 1930s saw a drastic reduction in creative freedom. This was in line with a general suspicion by the state of all independent lines of thought. Creativity had to serve the immediate needs of the government (called '*Partiinost*' – Party spirit). What emerged from this was 'Socialist Realism'.

Socialist Realism replaced the abstract experimental work of the 1920s with stereotypical art forms designed to convey immediately obvious pro-Soviet messages. Considerable effort was employed to create striking and inspiring posters and sculptures which represented Soviet society as happy and

Figure 6
Socialist Realism poster, showing Stalin and workers united in the industrialisation of the USSR.

Figure 7
Socialist Realism painting by I. Toidze showing Stalin talking to workers at the opening of a hydroelectric power station.

healthy and engaged in constructive and exciting industrial work. Most of the themes were taken from industry or collective farms. Often Stalin was included in set-piece artwork showing a people and leader harmoniously working towards a new Russia (see Figures 6 and 7).

Novels idealised the heroic achievements of the Five-Year Plans and plots became highly stereotyped. In 1932 the Union of Soviet Writers was established (replacing the previous body, the RAPP) to ensure that books followed the official Party line. The state's control of the arts was in one sense successful as it made them totally subservient to the needs of the regime. On the other hand such limitation of creative talent was frustrating and, in the post-war period, produced large numbers of dissident writers as its legacy.

Studying 'Soviet society in the 1930s'

1 In order to evaluate the way the creative arts were manipulated by the Soviet state, study four examples of the art of the 1930s. Two are provided in this section, another in section 3 (Five-Year Plans); find another example yourself.

For each example identify the message(s) it was meant to convey; analyse the techniques used to achieve those aims; evaluate how successfully it conveys the message(s).

2 After examining the issues outlined in this chapter makes outline essay notes to answer the following question:

'How successful was Stalin's drive to transform Soviet society, 1929–39?'

Identify the areas that require analysis in order to answer the question; examine evidence for Stalin's possible motivation and the background to his activities; make an assessment regarding the extent to which he achieved a transformation of society in the USSR.

6 Issues and interpretations

How has the history of the USSR under Stalin been interpreted by historians?

Key points

◆ Traditional interpretations of Soviet history
◆ How has recent 'openness' changed what evidence is available?
◆ What are the disagreements between 'Intentionalists' and 'Revisionists'?

What has been the evidence for traditional interpretations of Soviet history?

The study of Soviet history is not static. As with all periods of history, there are significant disagreements amongst historians. However, in the case of the history of the USSR, there are much more fundamental problems in the evidence historians can use. The disagreements among historians of the USSR arise from two main areas. Firstly, the secretive nature of Soviet government has meant that there is no absolute consensus about what makes up the basic data for the period. This is a fundamental issue and it shows itself in disagreements, for example, about the numbers of people killed during the purges; whether a person purged from the Party, or military, should automatically be considered a casualty; the production figures and achievements of the Five-Year Plans. This is a crucial issue as it constitutes the basis for interpretations of Soviet history.

The second area of disagreement arises naturally from the first. Since there is not always a consensus about what makes up the raw evidence, it is hardly surprising that differences in interpretation divide historians into different 'camps'. This is a common feature of all historical study but has become a particularly divisive feature in studies of the USSR.

Since the mid-1980s many of the long-established interpretations of events in the USSR have been challenged. This process has accelerated during the 1990s, as new evidence comes to light. In return, historians representing more traditional views have responded to the new wave of opinions by restating their views but with the assistance of new evidence.

Emigré, defector and samizdat writings

Many traditional interpretations were based on a vast amount of evidence but often in the form of émigré, or defector memoirs. These writings were produced by people who, for one reason or another, had fled the USSR. Many of these people had experienced some of the worst brutalities of Stalinist government. These writings seemed to offer a way by which western historians could explore the experiences of citizens of the USSR.

Another, and similar source of information lay in collections of evidence which circulated illegally in the USSR. These, so-called *samizdat* writings, were produced by historians and writers still living in the USSR. Because they did not conform to the official Communist Party version of events these writings were produced 'underground' and a number became available in the West. Authors of such material often suffered persecution for collecting and distributing such illegal information.

Problems with traditional sources of evidence

There are two main problems with these classes of evidence. Firstly, they were often, by nature, critical of the regime. Accounts by critics of the Communist government – whether originating inside, or outside, the USSR – tended to focus on the most negative features of Communist rule. In addition to this, they suffered from the fact that they were produced by people from outside the ruling élite. As such they had no access to the real sources of data needed to form a clear view of why events unfolded as they did.

To really untangle the motives of Stalin and the Politburo, for example, it is necessary to examine official documents, government minutes and resolutions. The producers of émigré and *samizdat* literature simply had no access to such information. It remained firmly in the hands of the Soviet government until the late 1980s. This severely weakened the reliability of their evidence regarding matters of government policy.

This does not mean that these sources provide no useful information. In fact they give vivid insights into the way government policy affected the lives of people in the USSR. In addition, they suggest ways in which people living at the time viewed these events. However, they rarely contain quantifiable statistical data, or offer insights into what was going on at the top of government.

Amongst the émigré/defector memoirs quoted by many western historians is the ex-NKVD officer, Alexander Orlov. A defector to the USA, he wrote in the 1950s and eventually worked for American intelligence. Despite the fact that he was in Spain during the Terror and not involved in the detailed planning of events his account has influenced many traditional interpretations.

Like Orlov, many other Russians whose works were quoted by western historians were not intimately involved in the top level of Stalin's government. Victor Kravchenko, often quoted, whilst involved in implementing the Five-Year Plans, was far from the centre of decision making.

Other émigrés were Trotskyists or Mensheviks. Whilst this in no way means their witness is invalid, it does mean that it has to be examined with great care. As well as living far from the events they described, their interpretations may well be coloured by their own political opposition to Stalin.

What has been the impact of glasnost on available evidence?

One of the problems facing western historians has been difficulty in getting access to primary sources from the USSR. This was caused by the Communist Party's reluctance to encourage open enquiry. For example, it took the

American historian Sheila Fitzpatrick from 1978 until 1985 to persuade the Lenin Library in Moscow to allow her to examine the Moscow and Leningrad telephone directories for 1937 and 1939!

Since 1985, the efforts of Gorbachev and his successors have made it possible to examine evidence once kept secret, or difficult to gain access to. This was one consequence of the policy of *glasnost*, or 'openness' in Soviet life. However, the use of archive sources does predate *glasnost*. In the 1950s Zbigniew Brzezinski and Merle Fainsod both used detailed documentation to support their studies. Fainsod, in particular, used the records of the Communist Party in Smolensk, which was captured by the Germans in 1941 and later fell into US hands. However, such sources of evidence were few. This has changed with *glasnost*.

What new evidence has emerged?

◆ Communist Party archives, particularly for local party branches and factory organisations.

◆ Mass graves such as those unearthed at Kuropaty and Bukovnya. These people were victims of the Terror.

◆ NKVD archives, giving data about the numbers executed. These have been explored by the Russian historians N. Dugin (1989) and V. N. Zemskov (1991).

◆ Population statistics from state archives, especially the 1939 census and local government registry offices which recorded births and deaths.

◆ Local press collections, giving details of what was going on far from the centres of power.

As the records of the Politburo and Central Committee for 1928–53, Stalin's personal archives and the more secret archives of the NKVD secret police become available Stalin's role in key decisions may become clearer. This process has already begun. However, there is a real possibility that many documents may have been destroyed.

'Intentionalists' versus 'Revisionists'

The use of pre-*glasnost* data led many historians to a view of Soviet society which may be summed up in the following way:

> The USSR suffered systematic and widespread repression; this repression was centrally organised by the Communist Party, which was dominated by Stalin. Soviet society was the passive victim of a strong state. Such a powerful state was 'totalitarian'. This means it had the power to actively control society and dominate most aspects of life.

Writers particularly associated with this perspective include: Hannah Arendt, Merle Fainsod, Robert Conquest, Robert Service, Roy Medvedev, Aleksandr Solzhenitsyn, Edvard Radzinsky, Dmitri Volkogonov. Since these viewpoints have been challenged, terms have been coined to describe these historians. These terms include 'Intentionalist' and 'Traditionalist'. Historians described by these terms do not, of course, share exactly the same views. However they tend to have certain common characteristics.

Many so called Intentionalist historians argue that some of the latest data from the ex-USSR supports their views. They point to the discovery of mass graves and documents revealing Stalin's knowledge of executions and his active encouragement of a policy of Terror. Some, like Robert Conquest, frankly reject the accusation that their opinions arose from anti-Soviet bias: "Such views [he suggests] could only be formed by ignoring, or actively rejecting the earlier evidence. This was accomplished by saying that those who produced it were opposed to Stalin and Stalinism and therefore prejudiced, and that some of the material was secondhand" (*The Great Terror, A Reassessment,* 1990).

Since the mid 1980s traditional viewpoints have been challenged and the historians responsible have been labelled 'Revisionists', 'Structuralists', or 'Decisionists' amongst other titles. In reality these are not titles that many would choose for themselves and they do not all think the same things. However, historians who share certain common features and might be called 'Revisionists' include: J. Arch Getty, Roberta Manning, Robert Thurston, Lynne Viola, Gabor Rittersporn, Stephen Wheatcroft.

J. Arch Getty has summed up the view of a number of historians who reject traditional interpretations: "The monstrosity of Stalin's crimes and a generation of Cold War attitudes have contributed to what would be considered sloppy and methodologically bankrupt scholarship in any other area of enquiry" (*Origins of the Great Purges,* 1985). According to this viewpoint the lack of detailed primary sources encouraged some historians to base their interpretations of the USSR on evidence which was inadequate, biased and flimsy. This, it is argued led these historians to adopt a distorted view of the USSR.

Such views were encouraged, it is sometimes suggested, by the anti-Communist views current during the Cold War. Sheila Fitzpatrick has commented that some, so-called Revisionist, historians "thought the traditionalists' figures [for purge victims] were exaggerated because of their anti-Soviet bias" and that such historians regarded writers like Conquest as "cold warriors" attacking the USSR (*Stalinist Terror, New Perspectives,* 1993).

Revisionist historians claim that the only reliable interpretations are those

Figure 7
Intentionalist *v.* Revisionist
interpretations

Characteristics of Intentionalist interpretations of the USSR	**Characteristics of Revisionist interpretations of the USSR**
◆ Leaders have long-term aims.	◆ Weak state unable to fully control society.
◆ Centralised decision-making.	◆ Many different, sometimes contradictory centres of power.
◆ Government dominates society.	
◆ Importance of individual leaders.	◆ Social pressures more important than individual leaders' ideas.
◆ Pressure for change from the 'top down'.	◆ Pressure for change from the 'bottom up'.
◆ New interpretations accused of minimising responsibility of Stalin and extent of suffering of the population.	◆ Opportunistic decision-making, rather than careful planning.
	◆ Far fewer victims of the terror than originally supposed.
	◆ Widespread support for the Communist government.
	◆ Old interpretations accused of being based on invalid, or inadequate evidence and anti-Communist bias.

based on detailed archive sources, many of which are only recently available. These new sources have led them to offer new interpretations. Some of the features of these new interpretations are shown in Figure 7.

Towards a new realism?

The apparent extremes of Intentionalists versus Revisionists can confuse the issue. This is because few of the historians hold views as extreme as they are sometimes accused of holding. What is clear is that things can be learned from both approaches.

The traditional (Intentionalist) approach reminds us that individuals, such as Stalin, can have a significant influence on events and policy. Whilst at times the evidence they quote may be focused on the experiences of a limited number of Soviet citizens, accounts from the victims of Stalin remind us of the human cost of Stalinism. Furthermore, their focus on centralised power provides a challenging explanation for how Soviet society was radically transformed.

On the other hand Revisionist historians are surely correct to remind us that powerful leaders are not the sole explanation for why events occur. Their analysis suggests that Stalin did not work from clear plans (other than the broadest of aims) but was instead a practical and opportunistic politician, who was flexible as well as brutal. They also remind us that the size and complexity of the USSR made it difficult for the government to dominate it and that competing groups often made government chaotic and confused. In addition, their evidence for widespread support for Stalin and many of his policies gives a persuasive explanation for his success in dominating Soviet society.

In short, a new realism, based on examining both extremes, leaves us with a picture of a complex society in which leaders tried to control but often could not dominate society and in which many ordinary people were active participants in many of the events that affected their lives. The picture that emerges does not minimise the suffering of the victims but it does insist that we look very critically at the evidence. In addition, it requires us to appreciate that government needs a great deal of active co-operation from the people and at the same time is often more chaotic and complex that we sometimes assume it to be.

Studying 'Issues and interpretations'

 1 In order to see how different approaches to a period of history occur it is necessary to study specific viewpoints. Below are some issues. By selecting work written by different historians it is possible to build up contrasting interpretations. When doing this ensure that:

a) You are using academic books rather than those written as school textbooks. The latter try to give both sides of the argument, so are less relevant for this exercise. Choose books written by some of the historians mentioned in this chapter.

b) Make a note of how their interpretations vary and what evidence they quote to back-up their viewpoints. Issues to use in this exercise:
◆ How many people died as a result of Terror in the 1930s?
◆ To what extent did Stalin control the Terror?
◆ Was collectivisation caused by economic, or political motives?

1: Titles of the secret police 1917–43

The name or initials used as the title of the Soviet secret police changed a number of times:

Cheka	1917–22
OGPU	1922–34
NKVD	1934–43

2: Results of collectivisation

The following table gives an indication of the grain harvest and livestock population before and after collectivisation.

	1929	1930	1931	1932	1933	1934	1935
Grain (*million tonnes*)	71.7	83.5	69.5	69.6	68.4	67.6	75.0
Cattle (*millions*)	67.1	52.5	47.9	40.7	38.4	42.4	49.3
Pigs (*millions*)	20.4	13.6	14.4	11.6	12.1	17.4	22.6
Sheep & goats (*millions*)	147.0	108.8	77.7	52.1	50.2	51.9	61.1

(From A. Nove, *An Economic History of the USSR*, 2nd ed.,1989)

3a: Achievements of the Five-Year Plans

The following are selected items from a wide range of industrial products.

Product	1928	1932	1937
Coal (*million tons*)	35.4	64.3	128.0
Oil (*million tons*)	11.7	21.4	28.5
Pig iron (*million tons*)	3.3	6.2	14.5
Steel (*million tons*)	4.0	5.9	17.7
Wool cloth (*million metres*)	97.0	93.3	108.3

(Figures from A. Nove, *An Economic History of the USSR*, 2nd ed.,1989)

3b: Working-class population of the USSR

	1928	1932	1937	1940
(in millions)	4.6	10.0	11.7	12.6

(From G. Hosking, *A History of the Soviet Union, 1917–1991,* 3rd ed.,1992)

4: The population of the Soviet Gulag, 1934–41

Estimates of the number of people imprisoned during the Terror vary enormously. These here are based on recently released secret police archives. (From work published by the Russian historian V. Zemskov in the Russian journal *Istoriia SSSR*, no. 5, 1991.) These figures cover prisoners in concentration camps of various kinds (the Gulag). Since statistics for people held in ordinary prisons are not included, the total number arrested would have been significantly higher. For example, in 1937 a further 545,000 people were in prison; in 1939 the additional number was 350,538.

1934	510,307	**1938**	1,881,570
1935	965,742	**1939**	1,672,438
1936	1,296,494	**1940**	1,659,992
1937	1,196,369	**1941**	1,929,729